U.S.A. TRAVEL GUIDES

OHIO

BY ANN HEINRICHS • ILLUSTRATED BY MATT KANIA

The Child's World®
childsworld.com

Published by The Child's World®
1980 Lookout Drive • Mankato, MN 56003-1705
800-599-READ • www.childsworld.com

Photo Credits
Photographs ©: iStockphoto, cover, 1, 8, 12, 20, 23,
32; Sonja CC2.0, 7; M. Reed/Wayne National Forest,
11; Mbr/MCT/Newscom, 15; Ron Thomas/iStockphoto,
16; Robert Lynn Ussery/Shutterstock Images, 19; Ken
LaRock/U.S. Air Force, 24; Amy Sancetta/AP Images, 27;
Carol M. Highsmith/Carol M. Highsmith Archive/Library
of Congress, 28; Shutterstock Images, 31, 37 (top), 37
(bottom); Kenneth Sponsler/Shutterstock Images, 35

ISBN 9781503819757
LCCN 2016961188

Printing
Printed in the United States of America
PA02334

Ann Heinrichs is the author of more than 100 books for children and young adults. She has also enjoyed successful careers as a children's book editor and an advertising copywriter. Ann grew up in Fort Smith, Arkansas, and lives in Chicago, Illinois.

About the Author
Ann Heinrichs

Matt Kania loves maps and, as a kid, dreamed of making them. In school he studied geography and cartography, and today he makes maps for a living. Matt's favorite thing about drawing maps is learning about the places they represent. Many of the maps he has created can be found in books, magazines, videos, Web sites, and public places.

About the
Map Illustrator
Matt Kania

*On the cover: Stop by the Rock and Roll
Hall of Fame in Cleveland.*

OUR OHIO TRIP

OHIO

Ready for a grand tour of Ohio? You'll be glad you came! It's chock-full of things to discover.

You'll explore caves and creep through forests. You'll learn to milk cows and make candles. You'll ride a boat pulled by a horse. You'll wander between massive military airplanes. You'll see how Super Bowl footballs are made. And you'll watch rats playing basketball!

There's much more to explore, so buckle up. You can follow that loopy dotted line. Or else just skip around. Ohio, here we come!

WELCOME TO
OHIO

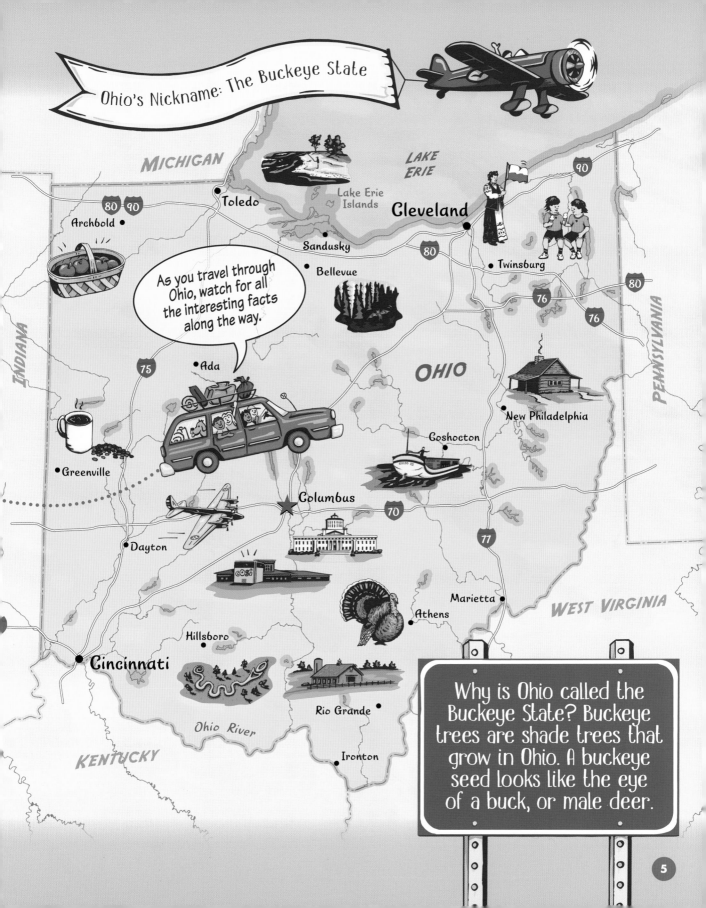

Lowest Temperature: Milligan February 10, 1899 −39°F (−39°C)

Highest Temperature: Gallipolis July 21, 1934 113°F (45°C)

LAKE ERIE

Lake Erie separates Canada and Ohio.

• Bellevue

It's really spooky down here! We can explore seven levels.

PENNSYLVANIA

INDIANA

Campbell Hill

West Liberty •

Milligan •

HIGHEST AND LOWEST POINTS
HIGHEST: Campbell Hill at 1,550 feet (472 m)
LOWEST: Along the Ohio River in Hamilton County at 455 feet (139 m)

Ohio Caverns is in West Liberty. It's the largest of Ohio's caves.

WEST VIRGINIA

Hamilton County

Ohio River

Gallipolis •

Ohio's caves were formed by underground streams. The water wore away the rock, leaving tunnels.

Lake Erie is the shallowest of the five Great Lakes. The others are Lakes Superior, Michigan, Huron, and Ontario.

KENTUCKY

SENECA CAVERNS IN BELLEVUE

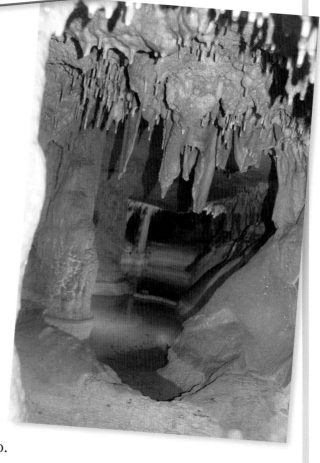

Peter and Henry were walking with their dog. The dog began chasing a rabbit. Both animals disappeared into a hole. Peter and Henry followed after them. Then kerplunk! The boys landed in a deep, underground cave. They had discovered Seneca **Caverns**. Now you can explore those caverns, too.

The Ohio River forms Ohio's southern border. Many other rivers flow south into the Ohio River. Some rivers flow north into Lake Erie. This lake borders northern Ohio.

Eastern Ohio is rugged and hilly. Rolling plains cover western Ohio. This region's rich soil makes great farmland.

Discover an underground pool at Seneca Caverns.

FUN ON THE LAKE ERIE ISLANDS

Ohioans love to visit the Lake Erie islands. They go camping, hiking, and picnicking there. They can also go fishing, boating, and swimming. Some islands even have caves to explore. Ohio's northeastern hills are great for hiking, too.

Some people enjoy watching team sports. Ohio sports fans have plenty to cheer about. Ohio is home to several sports teams. They play football, baseball, basketball, hockey, and soccer. College football fans are proud of the Buckeyes. They're the Ohio State University's champion football team.

Look for the West Sister Island Lighthouse on Lake Erie!

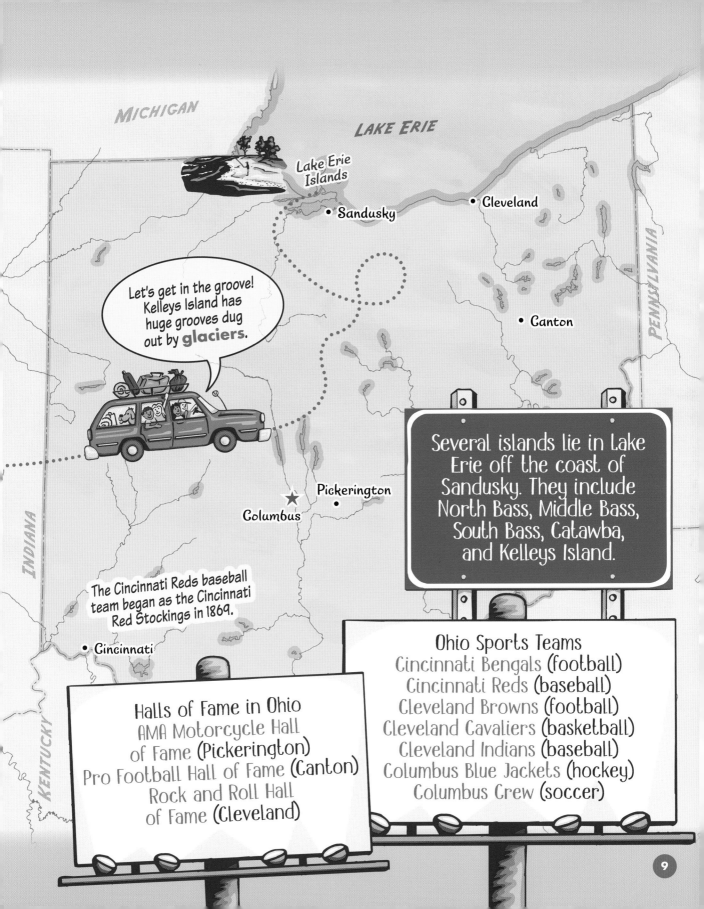

MICHIGAN

LAKE ERIE

Lake Erie Islands

• Sandusky

• Cleveland

PENNSYLVANIA

• Canton

Let's get in the groove! Kelleys Island has huge grooves dug out by **glaciers**.

Several islands lie in Lake Erie off the coast of Sandusky. They include North Bass, Middle Bass, South Bass, Catawba, and Kelleys Island.

Pickerington
Columbus

INDIANA

The Cincinnati Reds baseball team began as the Cincinnati Red Stockings in 1869.

• Cincinnati

KENTUCKY

Ohio Sports Teams
Cincinnati Bengals (football)
Cincinnati Reds (baseball)
Cleveland Browns (football)
Cleveland Cavaliers (basketball)
Cleveland Indians (baseball)
Columbus Blue Jackets (hockey)
Columbus Crew (soccer)

Halls of Fame in Ohio
AMA Motorcycle Hall
of Fame (Pickerington)
Pro Football Hall of Fame (Canton)
Rock and Roll Hall
of Fame (Cleveland)

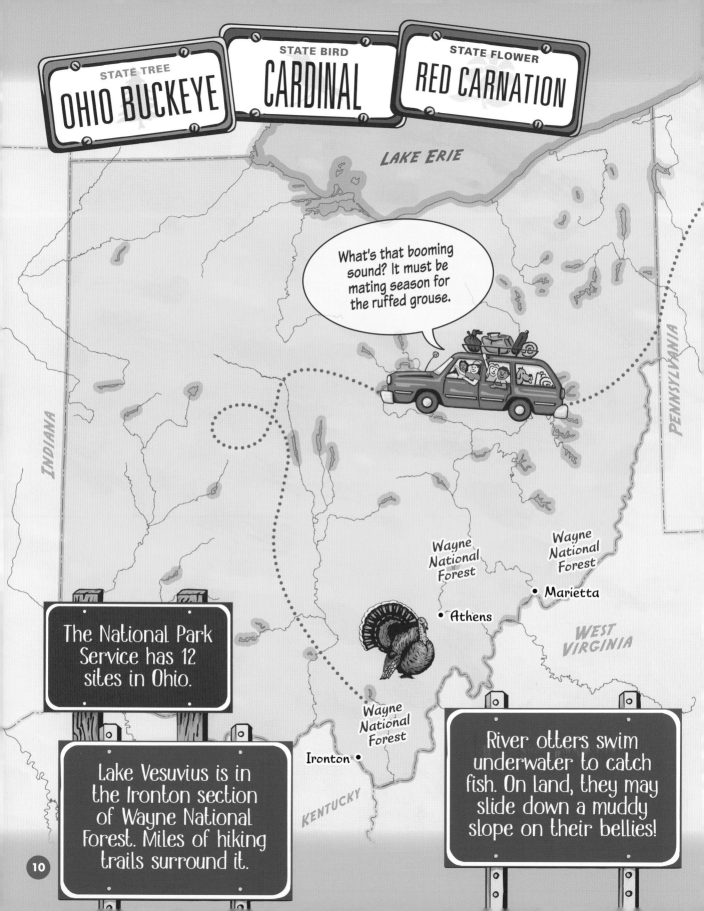

STATE TREE
OHIO BUCKEYE

STATE BIRD
CARDINAL

STATE FLOWER
RED CARNATION

LAKE ERIE

What's that booming sound? It must be mating season for the ruffed grouse.

INDIANA

PENNSYLVANIA

Wayne National Forest

Wayne National Forest

• Marietta

• Athens

WEST VIRGINIA

The National Park Service has 12 sites in Ohio.

Wayne National Forest

Ironton •

Lake Vesuvius is in the Ironton section of Wayne National Forest. Miles of hiking trails surround it.

KENTUCKY

River otters swim underwater to catch fish. On land, they may slide down a muddy slope on their bellies!

WATCHING WILDLIFE IN WAYNE NATIONAL FOREST

Walk softly, facing the wind. Then the animals won't hear or smell you. You'll see deer grazing on the forest floor. Wild turkeys strut through the leaves. Watch out! You might even see bobcats or bears.

River otters live near streams. They float on their backs in the water. If it's spring, you might spot ruffed grouse. They flutter and beat their wings. This makes a loud drumming sound. Males do this to attract a mate.

You're wandering through Wayne National Forest. It has three big sections. They're near Marietta, Athens, and Ironton. All three are great for watching animals!

Watch bumblebees buzz from flower to flower at Wayne National Forest.

THE SERPENT MOUND NEAR HILLSBORO

The Serpent Mound winds through the forest. You can see it best from the air. It looks like a giant snake. The Adena or the Fort Ancient peoples likely built it. They were both mound-building Native American groups. Scientists do not know the exact age of the mound. It may have been built as late as 1500 AD or as early as 300 BC. The builders piled up soil to form the long mound. Ohio has many **prehistoric** sites. People who lived there built huge **earthworks**.

French explorers were the first Europeans in Ohio. They came from Canada, to the north. British **colonists** moved in from the Atlantic coast, too. The French and British fought for control over North American lands. They made peace after the British won in 1763.

Tall grass shows visitors where the serpent lies.

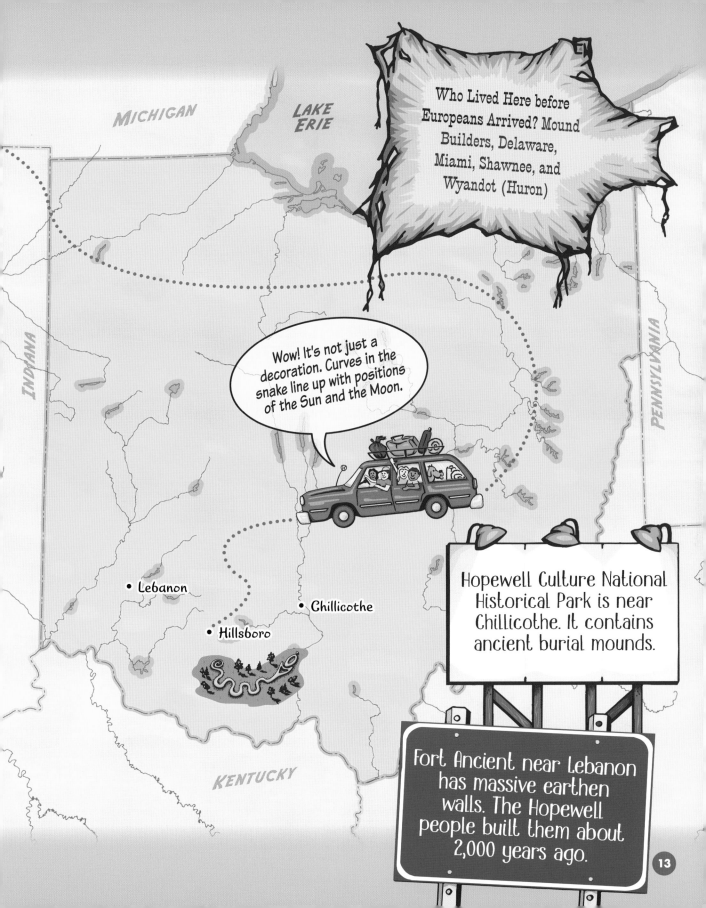

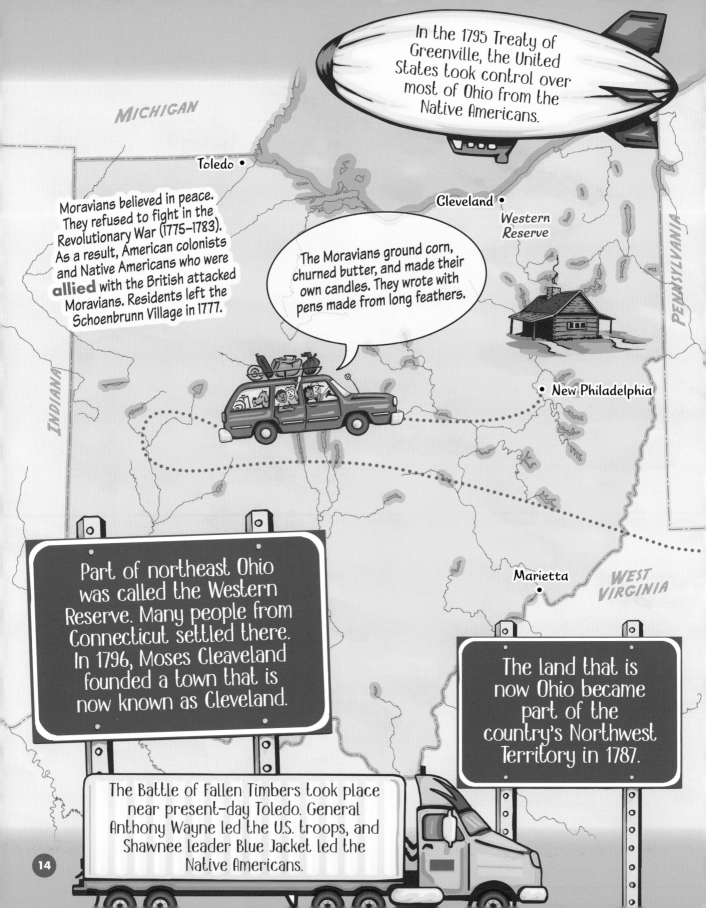

In the 1795 Treaty of Greenville, the United States took control over most of Ohio from the Native Americans.

MICHIGAN

Toledo •

Moravians believed in peace. They refused to fight in the Revolutionary War (1775–1783). As a result, American colonists and Native Americans who were **allied** with the British attacked Moravians. Residents left the Schoenbrunn Village in 1777.

Cleveland •

Western Reserve

The Moravians ground corn, churned butter, and made their own candles. They wrote with pens made from long feathers.

PENNSYLVANIA

INDIANA

• New Philadelphia

Part of northeast Ohio was called the Western Reserve. Many people from Connecticut settled there. In 1796, Moses Cleaveland founded a town that is now known as Cleveland.

Marietta

WEST VIRGINIA

The land that is now Ohio became part of the country's Northwest Territory in 1787.

The Battle of Fallen Timbers took place near present-day Toledo. General Anthony Wayne led the U.S. troops, and Shawnee leader Blue Jacket led the Native Americans.

SCHOENBRUNN VILLAGE NEAR NEW PHILADELPHIA

Log cabins look out over the cornfields. Crude log fences surround the land. A quiet, shady area is called God's Acre. It's a 200-year-old cemetery. You're visiting Schoenbrunn Village. **Missionaries** called Moravians settled there in 1772. They tried to spread Christianity to the Delaware Native Americans.

Settlers founded the town of Marietta in 1788. The Delaware, Miami, Ojibwe, Ottawa, and Shawnee fought to keep the settlers from taking over their lands. The U.S. army destroyed tribes' crops and homes. The two sides met at the Battle of Fallen Timbers in 1794. The U.S. army defeated the Native Americans. They forced the Native Americans to give up most of their Ohio lands in the Treaty of Greenville.

Schoenbrunn Village has 17 log buildings.

Learn to milk a cow. Wash clothes on an old scrub board. Chat with the broom maker, blacksmith, and other folks. Need a basket for your apples? Just stop by the basket maker's!

You're visiting Historic Sauder Village. It shows how Ohio **pioneers** lived.

Ohio grew fast in the 1800s. Thousands of settlers poured in. Some started farms by the Ohio River.

Farmers shipped their goods on the river. Those goods then traveled out of the state to the Mississippi River. Then they went south to New Orleans.

There are still many farms in Ohio today.

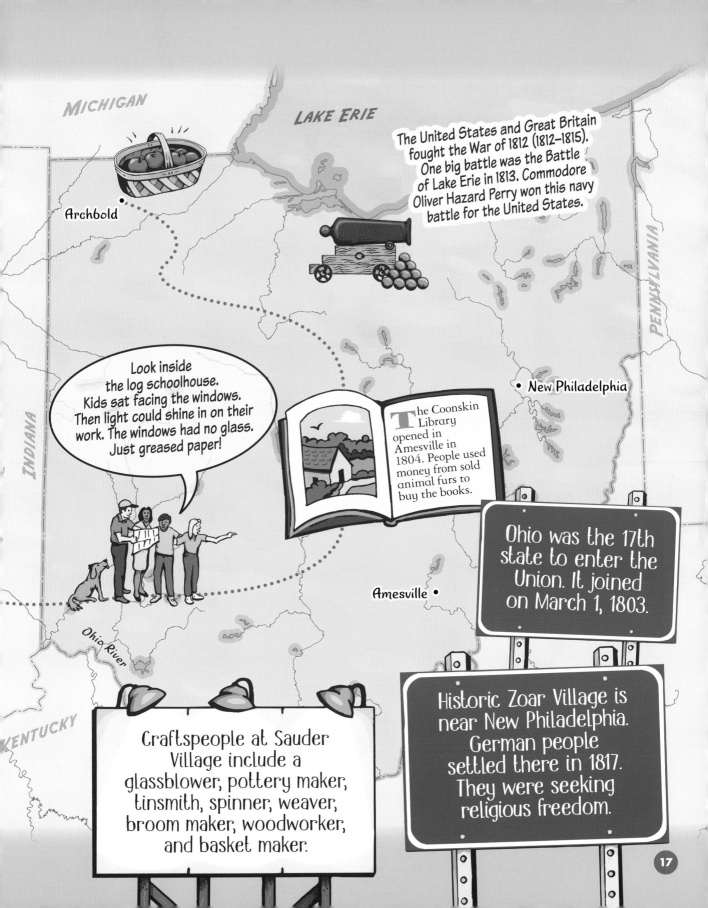

MICHIGAN

LAKE ERIE

The United States and Great Britain fought the War of 1812 (1812–1815). One big battle was the Battle of Lake Erie in 1813. Commodore Oliver Hazard Perry won this navy battle for the United States.

Archbold

PENNSYLVANIA

• New Philadelphia

INDIANA

Look inside the log schoolhouse. Kids sat facing the windows. Then light could shine in on their work. The windows had no glass. Just greased paper!

The Coonskin Library opened in Amesville in 1804. People used money from sold animal furs to buy the books.

Ohio was the 17th state to enter the Union. It joined on March 1, 1803.

Amesville •

Ohio River

KENTUCKY

Craftspeople at Sauder Village include a glassblower, pottery maker, tinsmith, spinner, weaver, broom maker, woodworker, and basket maker.

Historic Zoar Village is near New Philadelphia. German people settled there in 1817. They were seeking religious freedom.

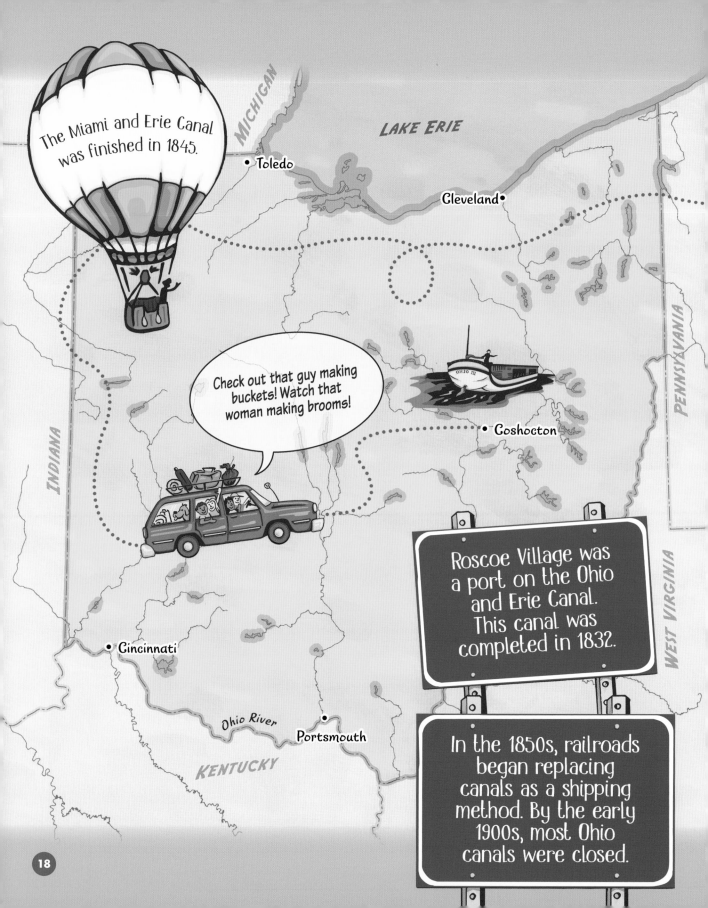

ROSCOE VILLAGE IN COSHOCTON

Visit the shopkeepers and craftspeople. Try your hand at dipping candles or making rope. Then climb aboard the **canal** boat. A horse on the bank pulls your boat along!

You're visiting Roscoe Village in Coshocton. It was a canal town in the 1830s. It shows how townspeople along the canals lived.

Ohio built canals to help move goods faster. One canal was the Ohio and Erie Canal. Its north end was at Cleveland, on Lake Erie. Its south end was at Portsmouth, on the Ohio River. The Miami and Erie Canal was another waterway. It ran between Toledo and Cincinnati.

Enjoy a stroll along the Ohio and Erie Canal.

Run in the Pierogi Dash, then snarf down some pierogies at the finish line. Watch the Polish Constitution Day Parade. People wear red and white, the colors of the Polish flag. You're visiting the Slavic Village! It's in Cleveland's Warszawa neighborhood. That's one of the state's Polish American communities.

Many **immigrants** settled in Ohio. Cleveland's **industries** made it an attractive new home. Now the city has dozens of **ethnic** neighborhoods. Some were settled by Polish or Hungarian immigrants. Puerto Ricans and Italians built communities there, too. So did people from Asia and the Middle East.

Pierogies can be topped with sour cream, tomato sauce, or many other things!

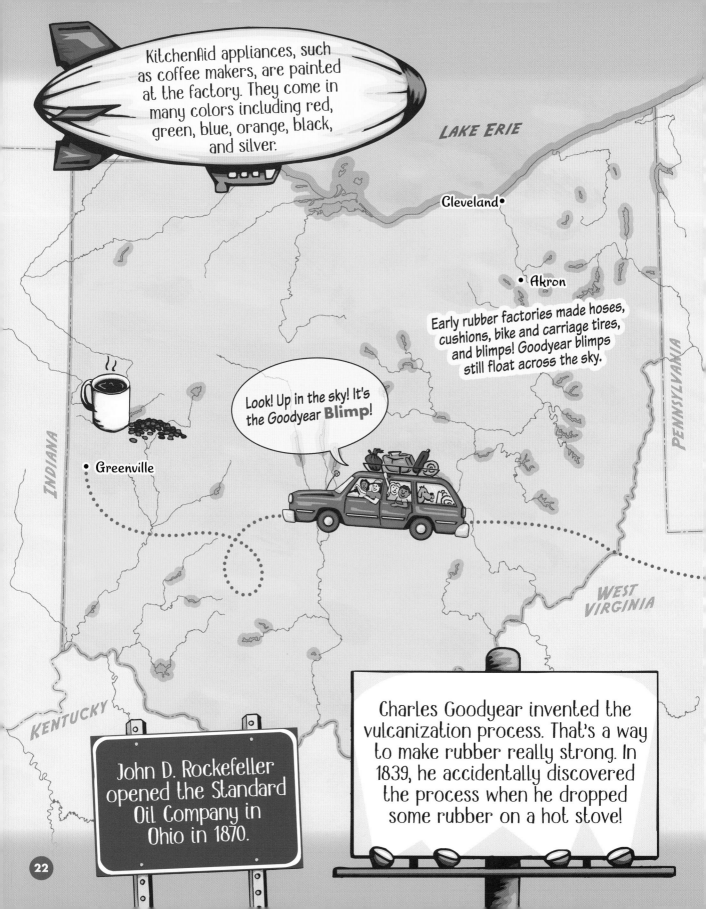

Kitchenaid appliances, such as coffee makers, are painted at the factory. They come in many colors including red, green, blue, orange, black, and silver.

LAKE ERIE

Cleveland•

•Akron

Early rubber factories made hoses, cushions, bike and carriage tires, and blimps! Goodyear blimps still float across the sky.

Look! Up in the sky! It's the Goodyear **Blimp**!

INDIANA

• Greenville

PENNSYLVANIA

WEST VIRGINIA

KENTUCKY

John D. Rockefeller opened the Standard Oil Company in Ohio in 1870.

Charles Goodyear invented the vulcanization process. That's a way to make rubber really strong. In 1839, he accidentally discovered the process when he dropped some rubber on a hot stove!

EXPERIENCE KITCHENAID IN GREENVILLE

Go back in time to see old KitchenAid appliances at the KitchenAid museum. Tour the KitchenAid factory to see how appliances are made. Watch appliances in action at the demo kitchen. You're enjoying the KitchenAid Experience in Greenville!

Factories have been important in Ohio for a long time. Many new industries developed in the mid-1800s. Ohio factories made foods, clothing, and farm tools. Cleveland became a center for steelmaking.

In 1839, Charles Goodyear found a way to make rubber strong. In 1870, Benjamin Goodrich opened Akron's first rubber factory. Akron's Goodyear Tire and Rubber Company opened later. Soon, new machines called automobiles became popular. Then Akron made millions of tires!

KitchenAid makes many countertop appliances including stand mixers.

DAYTON'S NATIONAL MUSEUM OF THE U.S. AIR FORCE

Do you like Snoopy in the *Peanuts* cartoons? Sometimes Snoopy flies an airplane. It's an early plane called a Sopwith Camel. You'll see a real Sopwith Camel in Dayton. It's at the National Museum of the U.S. Air Force. You'll see dozens of military airplanes there.

Ohio is proud of its flight history. The Wright brothers lived and worked in Dayton. They invented the first airplane. Astronaut Neil Armstrong was born in Wapakoneta. He was the first person to walk on the Moon. Ohioan John Glenn was another astronaut. He was the first U.S. astronaut to **orbit** Earth.

The Space Gallery at the National Museum of the U.S. Air Force has space vehicles that the Air Force made.

John Glenn orbited Earth in 1962. He was a U.S. senator from 1975 to 1999.

LAKE ERIE

Cleveland•

Oh, boy! We can sit in a **cockpit** and practice takeoffs and landings! Then we'll watch an awesome IMAX movie!

• Wapakoneta

PENNSYLVANIA

INDIANA

Dayton •

The National Museum of the U.S. Air Force is at Wright-Patterson Air Force Base. On the base is a field where the Wright brothers tested their airplanes.

Orville and Wilbur Wright made their first successful airplane flight in 1903 at Kitty Hawk, North Carolina.

WEST VIRGINIA

KENTUCKY

The John H. Glenn Research Center is in Cleveland. This center develops engines for aircraft and spacecraft.

Neil Armstrong walked on the Moon in 1969. The Armstrong Air and Space Museum is in Wapakoneta.

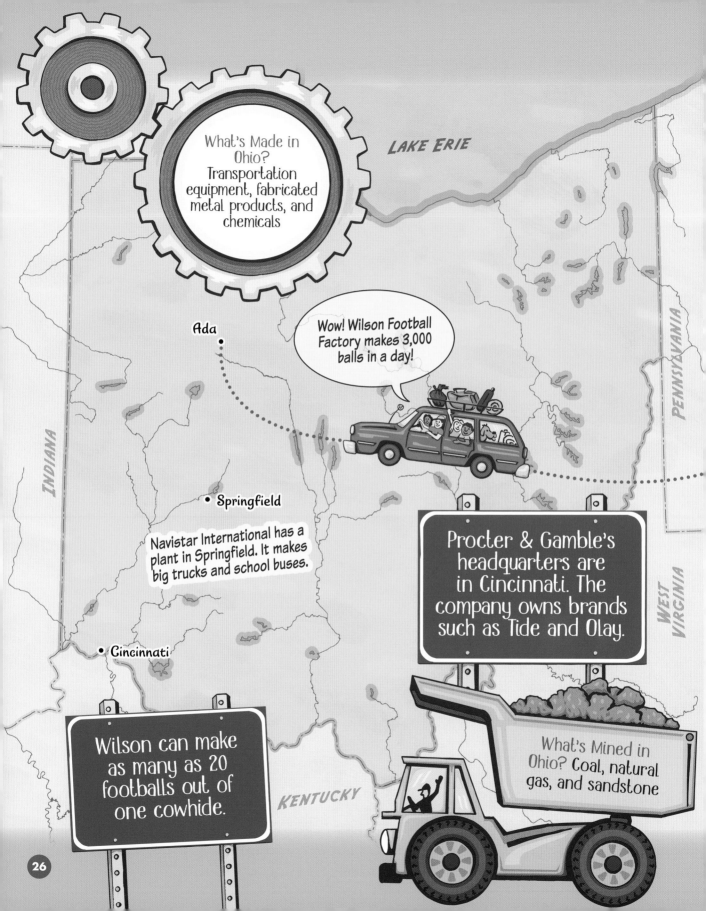

TOURING THE WILSON FOOTBALL FACTORY IN ADA

Do you like football? Then you'll love the Wilson Football Factory. Footballs are made here. Sewing machines churn away. Each ball is made by hand. Workers sew, cut, stitch, or lace. Some of these footballs are used in the NFL and even in the Super Bowl!

Manufacturing is a big industry in Ohio. The top factory goods are transportation equipment. That includes cars and trucks. Chemicals are another important factory product. Those include paint and cleaning products. Ohio also makes foods. Some food plants make soup, yogurt, or pizzas!

A worker sews a Super Bowl football.

THE STATE CAPITOL IN COLUMBUS

Walk inside the massive state capitol. Then look up. High overhead is a design in stained glass. It's the state seal. It shows a golden sun rising over mountains. A river flows beneath the mountains. There's a field and bundles of wheat and arrows. It's great to see this on a sunny day. The colors are dazzling!

The capitol houses many state government offices. Ohio's government has three branches. The governor heads one branch. This branch sees that laws are carried out. Another branch makes laws for the state. Judges make up the third branch. They listen to cases in courts. They decide whether someone has broken the law.

The Ohio capitol has a map of Ohio on the floor of the Map Room.

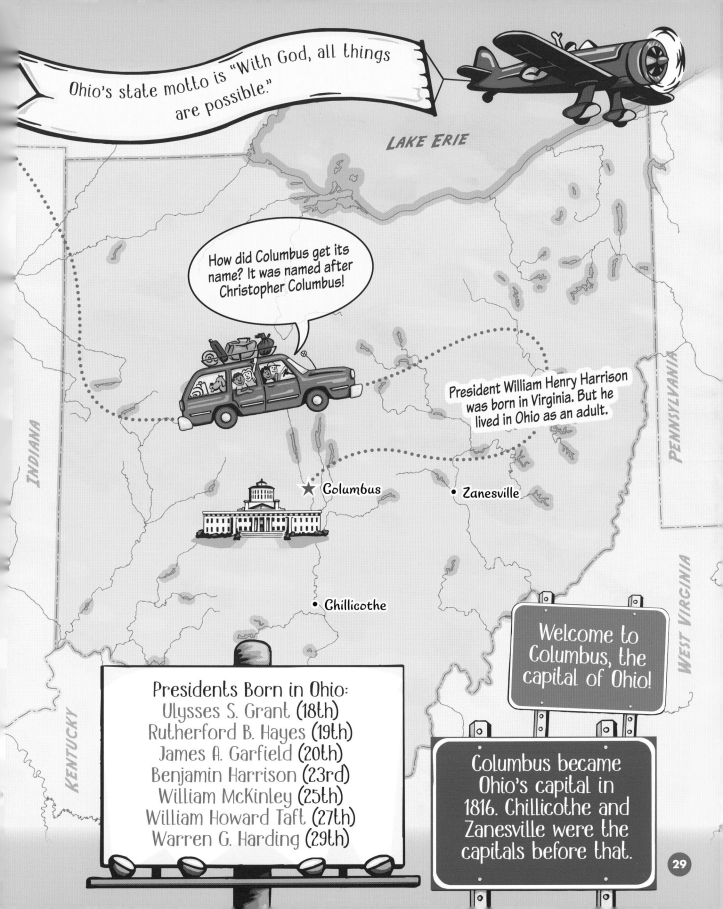

Ohio's state motto is "With God, all things are possible."

LAKE ERIE

INDIANA

PENNSYLVANIA

KENTUCKY

WEST VIRGINIA

How did Columbus get its name? It was named after Christopher Columbus!

President William Henry Harrison was born in Virginia. But he lived in Ohio as an adult.

★ Columbus

• Zanesville

• Chillicothe

Presidents Born in Ohio:
Ulysses S. Grant (18th)
Rutherford B. Hayes (19th)
James A. Garfield (20th)
Benjamin Harrison (23rd)
William McKinley (25th)
William Howard Taft (27th)
Warren G. Harding (29th)

Welcome to Columbus, the capital of Ohio!

Columbus became Ohio's capital in 1816. Chillicothe and Zanesville were the capitals before that.

29

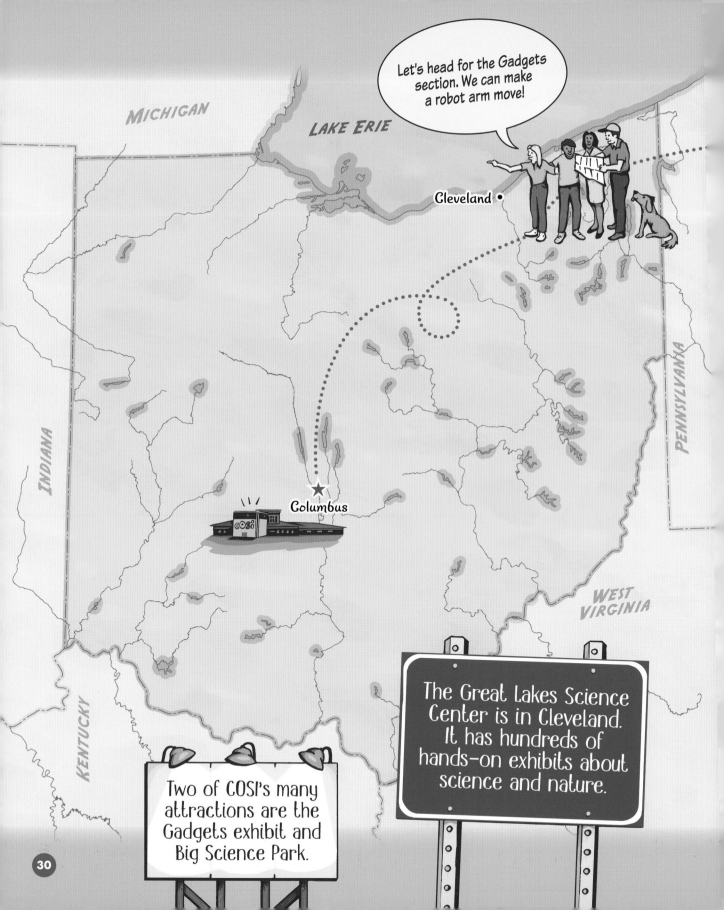

Let's head for the Gadgets section. We can make a robot arm move!

Two of COSI's many attractions are the Gadgets exhibit and Big Science Park.

The Great Lakes Science Center is in Cleveland. It has hundreds of hands-on exhibits about science and nature.

COLUMBUS'S CENTER OF SCIENCE AND INDUSTRY

Watch a team of rats play basketball. Feel electricity surging through your body. It makes your hair stand straight out!

You're exploring Columbus's Center of Science and Industry. It's called COSI for short. At COSI, you don't just look at stuff. You get involved! You try out science ideas yourself. Then you see how science laws work.

You'll learn about weather and electricity. You'll explore your own body and mind. And you'll discover the science secrets behind fireworks!

Trying to find COSI? Look for the big tree sculpture out front!

THE BOB EVANS FARM FESTIVAL IN RIO GRANDE

Pet the farm animals. See the sheep get their wool cut off. Then enter the pie-eating contest. It's the Bob Evans Farm Festival!

This is one of Ohio's many farm celebrations. Farmers in Ohio are pretty busy. Farmland covers about half the state. Soybeans and corn are the top farm products. Ohio is a leader in growing both crops.

Ohio's dairy farmers raise cows for their milk. Many farmers raise beef cattle, hogs, and sheep. Bob Evans raised hogs on his farm. He turned them into delicious sausage! The Bob Evans Farm carries on his legacy.

Cutting a sheep's wool is called shearing.

MICHIGAN

LAKE ERIE

The lowlands along Lake Erie are very fertile. Farmers there grow herbs and strawberries.

INDIANA

Let's take a horse-drawn wagon ride! Let's enter the horseshoe toss! Let's watch the chainsaw wood-carvers!

PENNSYLVANIA

Johnny Appleseed (1774-1845) was a pioneer hero. He wandered through Ohio planting apple trees. His real name was John Chapman.

★ Columbus

The state fair is held in Columbus in late July through early August each year.

WEST VIRGINIA

Rio Grande

What Does Ohio Raise?
Soybeans, corn, and milk

Bob Evans began making and serving sausage in 1946. He opened the original Bob Evans Restaurant in 1962. Now several hundred restaurants carry his name.

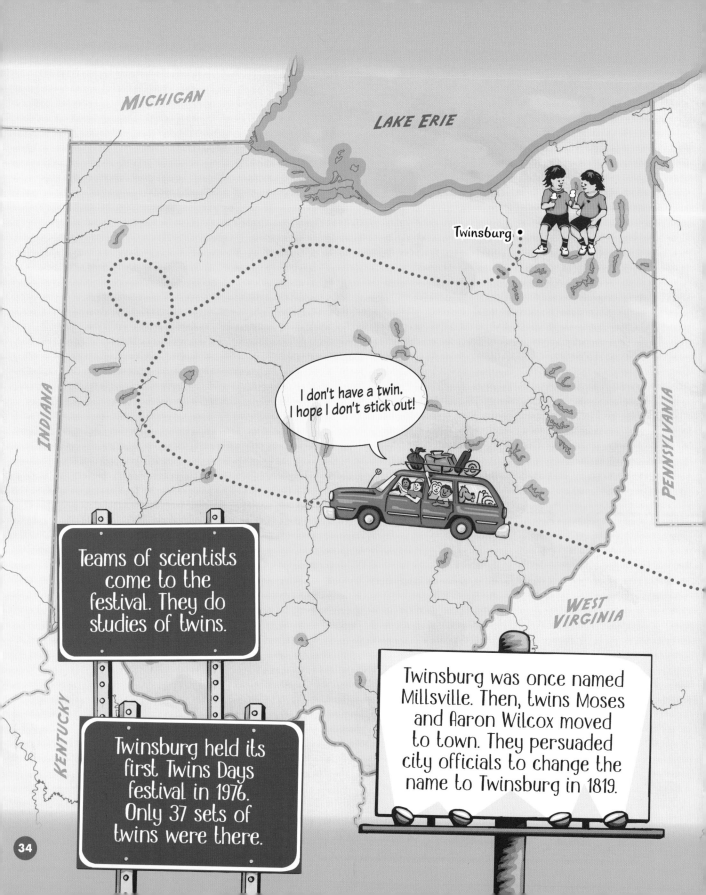

TWINS DAYS IN TWINSBURG

Are you seeing double? No. You've just wandered into the Twins Days festival! It's the world's largest gathering of twins. And it happens every August in Twinsburg!

Thousands of sets of twins attend every year. They march in the Double Take Parade. They take part in the Twins' Talent Show. And they enter some fun contests.

Triplets and quadruplets are welcome, too. What about people who were not multiple-birth babies? Can they attend? Of course. They just pay more to get in!

Twins can march in a parade at Twins Days!

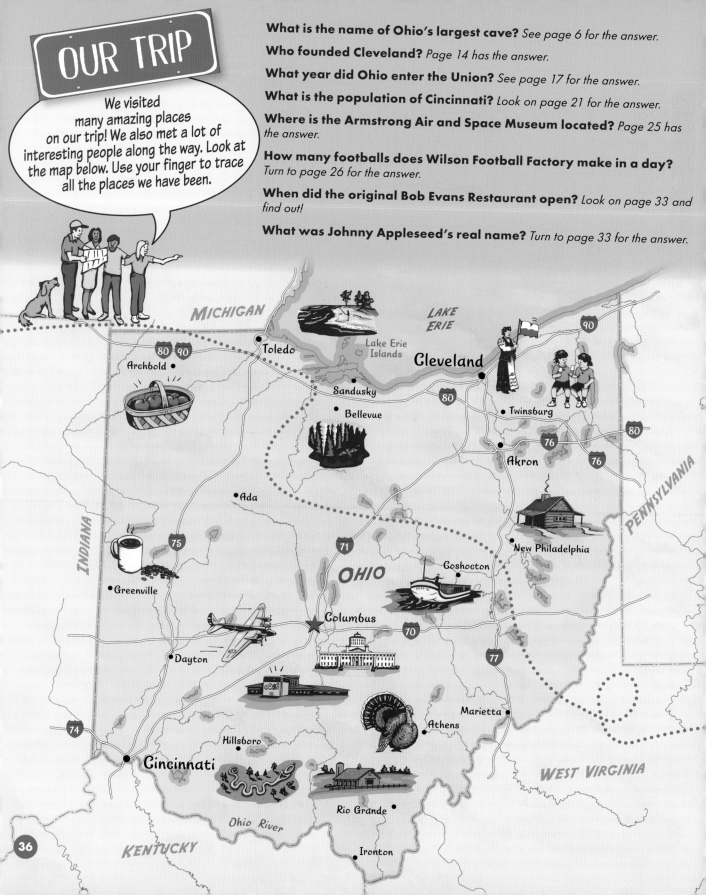

OUR TRIP

We visited many amazing places on our trip! We also met a lot of interesting people along the way. Look at the map below. Use your finger to trace all the places we have been.

What is the name of Ohio's largest cave? *See page 6 for the answer.*

Who founded Cleveland? *Page 14 has the answer.*

What year did Ohio enter the Union? *See page 17 for the answer.*

What is the population of Cincinnati? *Look on page 21 for the answer.*

Where is the Armstrong Air and Space Museum located? *Page 25 has the answer.*

How many footballs does Wilson Football Factory make in a day? *Turn to page 26 for the answer.*

When did the original Bob Evans Restaurant open? *Look on page 33 and find out!*

What was Johnny Appleseed's real name? *Turn to page 33 for the answer.*

MICHIGAN

LAKE ERIE

Toledo

Archbold

Lake Erie Islands

Cleveland

Sandusky

Bellevue

Twinsburg

Akron

Ada

New Philadelphia

INDIANA

PENNSYLVANIA

Greenville

OHIO

Goshocton

Columbus

Dayton

Marietta

Athens

Hillsboro

Cincinnati

Rio Grande

WEST VIRGINIA

Ohio River

Ironton

KENTUCKY

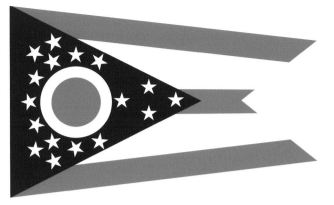

State flag

State seal

STATE SYMBOLS

State animal: White-tailed deer

State beverage: Tomato juice

State bird: Cardinal

State flower: Red carnation

State fossil: *Isotelus* (trilobite)

State gemstone: Ohio flint

State insect: Ladybug

State poetry day: Third Friday in October

State reptile: Black racer (snake)

State rock song: "Hang On Sloopy"
by Bert Berns and Wes Farrell

State tree: Ohio buckeye

State wildflower: Large white trillium

STATE SONG

"BEAUTIFUL OHIO"

Words by Wilbert McBride (earlier, original words by Ballard MacDonald), music by Mary Earl

I sailed away;
Wandered afar;
Crossed the mighty restless sea;
Looked for where I ought to be.
Cities so grand, mountains above,
Led to this land I love.

Chorus:
Beautiful Ohio, where the golden grain
Dwarf the lovely flowers in the summer
   rain.
Cities rising high, silhouette the sky.
Freedom is supreme in this majestic land;
Mighty factories seem to hum in tune, so
   grand.
Beautiful Ohio, thy wonders are in view,
Land where my dreams all come true!

That was a great trip! We have traveled all over Ohio! There are a few places that we didn't have time for, though. Next time, we plan to visit Cedar Point in Sandusky. We can ride the roller coasters and swim at Soak City! The amusement park also features live shows and a miniature golf course.

FAMOUS PEOPLE

Armstrong, Neil (1930–2012), astronaut, the first man to walk on the Moon

Berry, Halle (1966–), actor

Biles, Simone (1997–), Olympic gymnast

Cartwright, Nancy (1959–), the voice of Bart Simpson

Curry, Stephen (1988–), basketball player

Edison, Thomas Alva (1847–1931), inventor

Garfield, James (1831–1881), 20th U.S. president

Grant, Ulysses S. (1822–1885), 18th U.S. president

Hamilton, Scott (1958–), Olympic figure skater

Hayes, Rutherford B. (1822–1893), 19th U.S. president

James, LeBron (1984–), basketball player

Legend, John (1978–), singer

Lin, Maya (1959–), artist

Martin, Dean (1917–1995), entertainer

Newman, Paul (1925–2008), actor

Oakley, Annie (1860–1926), markswoman

Roethlisberger, Ben (1982), football player

Spielberg, Steven (1946–), film director

Tecumseh (1768–1813), Shawnee chief

Wilson, Russell (1988–), football player

Wright, Wilbur (1867–1912), **Orville** (1871–1948), aviation pioneers

Young, Cy (1867–1955), baseball player

WORDS TO KNOW

allied (AL-ide) people or groups of people working together toward a common goal

blimp (BLIMP) a gas-filled aircraft with no wings

canal (kuh-NAL) a long, narrow waterway dug by humans

caverns (KAV-ernz) caves

cockpit (KOK-pit) the part of an aircraft where the pilot sits

colonists (KOL-uh-nists) people who settle a new land for their home country

earthworks (URTH-wurks) large structures built out of soil

ethnic (ETH-nik) relating to a person's race or nationality

glaciers (GLAY-shurz) sheets of ice that move like flowing rivers

immigrants (IM-uh-gruhnts) people who leave their home country and move to another country

industries (IN-duh-streez) types of business

missionaries (MISH-uh-ner-eez) people who move somewhere to spread their religion

orbit (OR-bit) to travel in a circular pattern around an object

pioneers (pye-uh-NEERZ) people who move into an unsettled land

prehistoric (pree-hih-STOR-ik) taking place before people began writing down their history

TO LEARN MORE

IN THE LIBRARY
Jerome, Kate Boehm. *Columbus and the State of Ohio: Cool Stuff Every Kid Should Know.* Charleston, SC: Arcadia, 2011.

Jones, Kadeem. *Shawnee.* New York, NY: PowerKids Press, 2016.

ON THE WEB
Visit our Web site for links about Ohio:
childsworld.com/links

Note to Parents, Teachers, and Librarians: We routinely verify our Web links to make sure they are safe and active sites. So encourage your readers to check them out!

PLACES TO VISIT OR CONTACT
Ohio History Connection
ohiohistory.org
800 E 17th Ave.
Columbus, OH 43211
800/686-6124
For more information about the history of Ohio

Tourism Ohio
ohio.org
PO Box 1001
Columbus, OH 43216
800/282-5393
For more information about traveling in Ohio

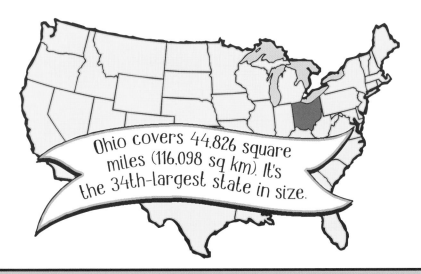

Ohio covers 44,826 square miles (116,098 sq km). It's the 34th-largest state in size.

INDEX

Bye, Buckeye State. We had a great time. We'll come back soon!